Rob Talbert's *Jagged Tune* is a gorgeous post-industrial lyric hymn to minimum-wage jobs: from corrections officer to pawn shop employee to cruise ship attendant to insurance certificate specialist to retail clerk to unemployed and back again, Talbert's poems—hewn from life experience—contrast the constraints of work with the ecstasy of nightclubs, their "feral engine" and "deep recess of liquor techno." "My life depends on night," he writes, and this is a nocturnal book that embraces the wonder of darkness, its broken song. I am awed by these poems—their unyielding eye, their deft music, their capacity for wisdom, and all the ways in which they illuminate facets of the American experience that we rarely see.

—*Erika Meitner*

How can the world be anything but a music made out of what we are, a jagged tune, a knife song, a wild blood and bone aria? In Rob Talbert's energetic, frightening, human, kinetic collection we can hear every note. I want to download this book into the musical score it is and listen to it whenever I'm alone but desperately need the world.

—*Matthew Dickman*

"Attention Customers: the store will close / in fifteen minutes. Sooner or later we all / return home." Thus begins Rob Talbert's *Jagged Tune*, and a jagged tune this collection of oddball dreams and dreamers it is. Imagine a poet barking his verses into a megaphone at the moon, picture "police lights open[ing] their eyes," your "sister ... swarmed by cops" and you'll get a taste for the dramas and requiems that unfold here. "Going back / to the start / is good," "Ingenious Ocean" begins; "The night is a dark dress I don't want / to see slip off. It's much too close / to the only thing I have in place of goodbye," this collection of elocutions ends.

— *Andrew McFadyen-Ketchum*

Jagged Tune steps to its reader with the gait of a boxer not accustomed to showing mercy. And yet, there's a hard-earned tenderness in these poems, an affirmation and hope tempered by the drab, brutal realities of minimum wage and high-security imprisonment. Part Whitman, part *The Threepenny Opera*, Talbert sifts through the wreckage of the everyday in search of the miraculous; what's amazing is how often he returns with the goods.

—*James Kimbrell*

"Attention Customers: the store will close / in fifteen minutes. Sooner or later we all / return home." Thus begins Rob Talbert's *Jagged Tune*, and a jagged tune this collection of oddball dreams and dreamers it is. Imagine a poet barking his verses into a megaphone at the moon, picture "police lights open[ing] their eyes," your "sister … swarmed by cops" and you'll get a taste for the dramas and requiems that unfold here. "Going back / to the start / is good," "Ingenious Ocean" begins; "The night is a dark dress I don't want / to see slip off. It's much too close / to the only thing I have in place of goodbye," this collection of elocutions ends.

— *Andrew McFadyen-Ketchum*

Jagged Tune steps to its reader with the gait of a boxer not accustomed to showing mercy. And yet, there's a hard-earned tenderness in these poems, an affirmation and hope tempered by the drab, brutal realities of minimum wage and high-security imprisonment. Part Whitman, part *The Threepenny Opera*, Talbert sifts through the wreckage of the everyday in search of the miraculous; what's amazing is how often he returns with the goods.

—*James Kimbrell*

Jagged Tune

Rob Talbert

MadHat Press
Asheville, North Carolina

MadHat Press
MadHat Incorporated
PO Box 8364, Asheville, NC 28814

The Library of Congress has assigned
this edition a Control Number of
2015900847

ISBN 978-1-941196-11-3 (paperback)

Text by Rob Talbert
Cover photograph by MadHat Press
Book and cover design by MadHat Press

www.MadHat-Press.com

First Printing

JAGGED TUNE

CONTENTS

Announcements

Attention customers: the store will close
in fifteen minutes. Sooner or later we all
return home. We close tonight
because all things end: songs, an empire,
most love, this sentence—ends.

Do not mistake this for proof of God.
Do not look the employees in the eye.
Some have been hit by a hurricane
of dreams. Your staring, your small talk,
remind them cement around
their ankles is drying, that a trillion
heartbeats have come and gone.
Minimum wage is a deeply planted knife.
Beeping registers haunt us in sleep.

Attention customers: please make
your final selections and bring them
to the front of the store for purchase.
This goes for lost children, the penniless,
the heartbroken, shoplifters, the man
in aisle nine exposing himself to his girlfriend.
What we do in our minds is a dark carnival
of mirrors and sharp candy, hidden
rampage where the fire burns hottest.
I've devastated friends and family.
Have no right to my anger, paralysis, starvation.
No desolate landscape to contend with.
But you drive safe, take care. Never forget
the promises you made to yourself.

Advice like that is safe. Most of the things
on our shelves can kill.

Cherries Becoming More like Cherries

Listen. The space you take up opens. Inhales.
Slow, like a praying monk at high altitude.
Balloons. Becomes a vowel with flesh pooling
out from the center. An *O* without a pit
and ready for a tongue. Say a name
and unleash fruit. Sweet as a body moving
toward a caller. Be especially easy
on asthmatics: their lives depend on every *yes.*
My life depends on night. The difference
between she and I: how easier a time
the wind has with her: with the windows
down. The tangle of roads tracing every
place skin flies. Above abrasion. Above
the legal posted limit. And the road is more
than a blur of mile markers and grass. Is,
for an instant, relevant. The Pacific is relevant
because it can be reached. Entered.
Occupied and made more. You are more
right here. And right here. You are more
than gravity because gravity has no body.
Has nothing to take its shape. Is kissless.
Will never call you for drinks. Even the dead
have shape, but gravity only tugs. On cherries.
On the feet while the car banks too fast
on turnpikes.

If you've ever driven far
enough from a city, then the largest *O*
you've ever seen is the arm of the galaxy.
Smooth and patient. A midnight

of presence. The miracle of enough time.
There is always an hour ready to hold you.
Like this one. A place in the room for refuge.
Molding all movements and memory. This.
Exactly. What has become of you.

Storming the Gates

Without night there's no guardian or shroud
for us to hide behind
when we fall back
into each other.

Remember the time you kissed a stranger
in the black-ink grass?
Remember smoke filling the car
in the church parking lot?
Remember whatever damn secrets you have?
Good.
Now wrap these treasures in barbed wire
because the world will tear them from you.
Time, money, family, a spouse, cops, teachers
will tear them from you.
Your boyfriend, your girlfriend
will tear them from you.

You gotta fight dirty before they do.
(And they will.)
You gotta shoot your own mother
on the lawn inside of you.

What my wife knows
and my friends know
and my boss knows
and the girls in laser skirts know
about me
would force me to live a thousand years.

This is my rebellion. My defense.
I scratch the night behind her ears
and stroll into vodka-kiss hotels.
I live as if an angel stole a bag of kindness
from the storage closet.

Now run. Go. Get out there.
Call everyone. Call it faith.
Call the glistening flames
between normal living
the first stutters of some new
and cosmic engine.

Job 1: Corrections Officer

Not all of them are murderers. Rapists. Thieves.
Those are the takers. The ones who, as children,
probably picked everything up off the ground.
Their ungentle hands eager and mud-caked
from digging, securing all findings in deep
pockets: bottle caps, a coin or two, small lizards,
eventually working their way up to people, though
that would come much later. Others need respite.
The drug users are givers. They can't give away
all blood carries. They think everything is a bomb
or wish it was, a benefactor of instant change,
ready to explode, loud and forever like it is inside
the heart. When you feel too much, peace is to live
sedated. We punish those who stop feeling.

I should've been in jail years ago; for the way I turned,
a wind vane changing direction, away from her voice.
Her gunfire pleas shelling my back as I strolled on
past the pawnshop and the city's only jazz club.
That was Corpus Christi, Texas. Years before snow
turned all the Virginia pines to silver in my window.
The cold, unbiased arc of the moon forcing glitter into
their evening gowns as it must've long before our ships
and planes were made of wood. It's just easier to get
around now. Leaving school and showing up back
home mid-semester, killing the best of my mother's
desires, took almost no effort at all.

How others define the world is a song you've never heard,
and they make it up as they go along, like Cole Porter high

on Chicago, or children playing a game they can't name.
I've got an idea for one: everyone go outside and find
something, rename it, emphasize your favorite way
to use it, then show someone else. I'll go first. You can
drive this all the way to the ocean, light your cigarettes
with it, listen to music, and make love for long hours
in the backseat while the sun watches you smile away
your sins. I call it a cell door.

Your turn.

Method

I took a cab down Commerce Street.
I took a cab and walked down from the mall.

There's a cover at Citrus.
I took a cab and the mall was closing.

Down Commerce Street I paid a cover.
I waved a cab down but it didn't stop.

The street lit up like a satin ribbon.
Citrus was lit like commerce of satin.

Her dress reigned in the land of small shoulders.
Her dress was caught in the cab door.

I walked to Citrus where there was a cover.
The mall was a dark box made of unbought things.

A ribbon went around my wrist.
A cab turned around on Commerce Street.

I walked to Citrus and the street was closing.
The sky was dark like a closed mall.

The sky was a cab door shut on a dress.
Her hips moved like ribbon blown into the street.

I drank from the mall of lit bottles.
The world will never end.

Rob Talbert

Baggage

There isn't much of a moon tonight. I guess she only feels
vaguely heroic. Secrets don't come whole either, but that's our

fault and no amount of velocity can get them all blooming
in the world. No one *really* spills their guts anymore. The dead

cities leave behind their ruined columns and bones and the wild
grass doesn't seem to mind, like it was already written

in the trillion bits of the universe as it was sewn together.
The struggle is that it feels natural to keep a morsel for yourself

before throwing the rest to the wolves. I plant an iris in my mind
to remember a woman at a party, but never do all the seeds

make it through. If you want a good memory you have to plant
in clusters. I drag this garden behind me everywhere and nobody

mentions it, my secret tool for comparable grief, to show others
I know how it feels to be left alone on a gravel lot in Arizona rain.

As usual, context is everything. Maybe thirty years from now
I'll realize why I've been a chained-up dog barking all night

at the neighbor's open window, but the archeologists are going
blind and I'm always so fiercely running out of time.

Ingenious Ocean,

are you still waiting
for life to crawl
back into you? I need
to be on time for that.
My body is mostly
you, after all. The tide comes
and goes like breath.
There are dreams
and people I want
to have back.
I lost them in hotels
and airports, in locker
rooms and bars.
I lost them in Vermont
fields and gas stations.
Going back
to the start
is good,
the first door,
the head of the ouroboros,
the place in the knot
where, if pulled,
will undo me and return.
Do you know where
they are, ocean?
My fragments? My
sleeplessness? I feel no
need to stop walking
just because the land
gives up. That's stubborn.

Rob Talbert

For the billionth time
        the sun came out.

Job 2: Cruise Ship Room Attendant

The American woman at the table screamed
at the Moroccan man who offered to buy her.
Screamed until her face
was a baboon's ass of scarlet.

The Moroccan asked her husband how much for her
in French
in spring
in well-ironed clothes reeking of cologne.

Even the birds heard her.

What do you think I am
a fucking souvenir? And you!
she said to her husband
Why aren't you beating him to death?

I leaned back in my chair and watched
the Moroccan go, strolling down
the sun-beat cobblestone

while the woman glared at her husband
and dipped the last of the bread
angrily
in the last of the olive oil.
The rocks on her hands gleamed
like a madman's ideas.
Her swollen bag of souvenirs
slumped below her slumped husband.

This man wasn't heartbroken,
just back-broken. A dull razor pushed around.
When I clean the mirror in their room
I imagine his reflection strangled nightly
by the lotion tubes and perfume bottles
overflowing on the dresser.

The Moroccan passed into the shadow
of a great mosque and the couple
edged back to the cruise ship. I doubt
the husband thinks often of the future.
I don't think he'd so easily
part with two thousand camels.

Crusoe, Wistful

Even if the ocean were for sale I'd never want the beach:
too ambiguous, too beginning-of-everything. Mountains
are as stubborn as you can get. Was there ever a compass
with more choices? An engine with fewer?
I remember all the names of the streets back home so
disappointingly quick. The faces of neighbors and their perfectly
square yards. Not at all how I imagine the torpid and scenic
spanning villages of eastern Europe, with their stone prisons
and pretty vowels rolling over tongues like countryside.
Not at all how I imagine Venus, warm under its blanket
of clouds and lost in perfect orbit.
          How agreeable its promise for rain.
Not at all how I imagine the bottom of the ocean, where nothing
is ever lonely or starves or hears *thank you* after saying *I love you.*

There's always forgiveness in somewhere else, and if you traveled
all the time you'd live without sin
          and in constant need of postcards,
but I'm sure you'd miss your bed and all its familiar stains, your
blender, the hopelessly married women at the office. My house
lacks a valley of hills and a winery. There should be a waterfall
in the next room that has nothing to do with my bathroom
          or the need
to impress neighbors. Of course there are images that form
in the ceiling's rough texture that I call miracles under my breath
but nothing expected is a miracle. Not even the horizon, waiting
for me beyond the front door.

What Practice Makes

The fence behind the house is clenched
teeth, where the sparrows and wildflowers
go to get eaten. The world keeps going but we don't
know for whom; our neighbor has been gone
years, either hit by a train or consumed with love.

Tired weather in the field defines the nature
of our hours with dark river clouds or the immortal
sun. Either way it gets us moving.

You hang the clothes on the line to get dusty and dry.
I've driven more nails into the leaning porch.
What quiet dinners we have. Blaming it all
on the busy day while our disillusioned neighbor
wanders out there, trying to get his life better.

I know there are dreams that wash over the bed,
and the horizon moves like a hula-hoop when no one
is looking. Sometimes I'm breathing a prayer so honest
it beats the heart for it, though I never know what
it says or what I should do next. Such is the way

of breath turning to wind. And how strange that renewal
is never pure. How skilled the hand is quietly turning
out the bedside lamp.

The Last Scene in Casablanca

Everything's already for sale
so I shoplifted color from the world,
brought you and I closer to static
on dead channels. Now I confuse
flowers with garbage. Now I can
say your eyes are the same as airplanes.

I still desire flight in this world, waiting
greedily for my turn, my path through
the city. We'll fly over the art gallery
and sigh, land in central park and try
to guess whether it's autumn. Some
will be angry. They'll say it's all over.

What demands ever sprang from metal?
That it never stay warm? Never only kiss you
in a crash? Strangely enough here we are,
held up and breathing, also in love but I
never did ask to be sure.

I've made up my mind to believe in gray,
to learn from this trip that the miracle
of the actions you take are what backgrounds
are made of. The city knew this years ago
and tried to tell me with sirens and barking
dogs but how could I realize? If the sky still exists

without blue then you can be a better lover
by taking me up into it, far away from all things
expected and made of traffic.

Rob Talbert

Finding Zero

At some point
you gave something soft
to a person now long absent.
A heart-shaped pillow.
A bear, maybe,
on a day reserved for holding bears.
That was years ago,
and that bear is surely buried
deep in the earth,
in the hierarchy of a landfill.
Deep as your memories
slide into unconscious action.
Deeper than you will ever be,
even when you are buried.
That's how far you reach.
And some nights
you must surely look up,
and whatever vague assertions
you have
about whatever poverties
you face
are just as far up
as that soft creature is down.
Call it hovering.
Call it how you are a cloud.
Call it how you, cloud, take
in the world and build.
Build with all the traffic and noise
and lost words and swell
with a heavy, angry darkness.

Dark as too far up
and too far down.
Full to the very ends of your might.
Then, your hand goes out.
Then it rains.

Rob Talbert

Job 3: Pawn Shop Employee

You must do it.
It's inescapable.
Even if you sit perfectly still
the blood, and heart and nerves
fire off like New Year's Eve sky.
Night chases you out
of the room. If not, then winter.
You must do it.
You must work.
Be subjected
to these forces and more.
Every second of existence is work.
Every second the world works you.

At the pawnshop I restock shelves
and move boxes and the beats
of my heart will never return.
Hours of my life worth
$8 each. Some reduce their lives
to a mere thousand bucks.
They pawn their wedding rings
and their grandmother's books.
They hand over pocket watches
that could drink you under the table.
These are my people and the people
I walk with. This is where the past
comes to die. I once had an idea
about the future, about its color
and textures, so when I say I want
the life I was promised, I mean

the life I promised myself. Most
of us can do no better against
the whims of an ancient current.
I know this. But in the dark corners
of my apartment I've started building.
A kind of shelter around the light.
Something to scratch the itch.
Something to prove my energy
comes from stars.

Rob Talbert

Praise to All Reused Vessels

This city is more significant in what it hides than what it is.
I'm missing the Pacific by living in San Antonio, or any mountain
that would obstruct other geniuses. I simply can't have a Lake Michigan
and an Alamo in the same evening walk to the restaurant.
The looming buildings and loud hospitals restrict my passage
into the map-promised countryside, and still I ignore the trees
in the park or a cactus leering by the highway. In my car is a bottle
with a note inside of it I promised a friend I'd throw
into the Gulf of Mexico. Here, it makes sense to substitute one
abyss for another. Here, my friend's last note to a long-gone girl
will be more gone, easing the sting when I tell him the bottle
floated back to shore.

I drift into the restaurant and spot my wife sitting alone
with a drink. Our skin collects the 87 colors from electric signs.
I believe in recycling, that we can use this color for infinite sunsets,
or how all the newspaper articles about theft and murder
keep the homeless warm at night on their park benches.
I imagine a city that sweeps up and stores all the confetti
left over from parades in case the stars vanish
or we blow them up. After all, the method in which I love now
is built from older, perfectly failed love, and I reuse the same few
lines and gestures. Whatever beauty is chosen will succumb
to the absence of other beauties. Selfishly, I want them all
in a bottle with a label that means something close to the future,
but the sun has already gone down and I am just a man.

Job 4: Unemployed

I.

The sirens go round and round, a changing mind in the facades.
Every street
is a different version of my past: on Navarro Boulevard I almost
went to war.
Houston Street is the two years my knee hurt from living
in nightclubs.

If I were a city I would be nothing like the architects'
blueprints and dreams. I would have more exits than doors.
Escape is that important.

The wind cools and grows eager. I watch videogame light pulsing
in the half-drawn curtained windows. A train whistle howls
its departure.
I shouldn't have ended up like this.

II.

I pay for a phone that doesn't ring. On my dresser
Springsteen's *Born in the USA* has enough dust on the sleeve
to prove February was here. I sense a forest, a place haunted
by wolves

and snow collecting on the banks. There is a kind of quiet
that existed before any city stood, the cleanest sound.
A television shows me what the world does: people arguing
about a blown call at Wrigley, how many Burrowing Owls

are left to kill.
The constant necessity of hunting placates the will. Somewhere
in somebody
is the rush of something happening, perhaps the fight of getting
born.

III.

A sculpted man at a sculpted desk bathes in the window-
reflected season:
his shirt means the sun exists, his fern in the corner dreams
of flowers.
I can see particles in the sunbeams rushing about in suspension,

diced and shoved by splendid trains carrying the city
about the city.
He interviews me neatly. The grass outside is neatly filed
and stored to the point
of being an empty thing. People often do this with their lives.
At night

I have been in new cars with engines made of other fantasies,
too fast for fast love, revving through my prime. Always, I am
en route
to the dream diner, open all night on any floating continent.

An Oven the Size and Shape of Texas

The drought is intact and drought inhabits me.
I am dust for miles, reading the branches
like wooden cursive contorting into sky.

I clasp my hands by a tired window screen
whose bottom-left corner has given up.
Dream catcher. Sun-beaten and tender as trust.
She filters the traffic of night air and arguments.

I've learned the yellow landscape spilling
from my mother's hands in the garden
was purposeful, an intended barrenness.

The land sang softly through the screen.
There is no science for this containment,
no reprieve from all heat occurring
in the million eons before I spilled into the world.

I go trick-or-treating in fake blood. I talk to girls
under cicada umbrellas. Their molted
shells still cling to houses, empty and split open
with memory.

I've waited for rain longer than rain
has existed. Two miles away, the stone walls
of Mission La Concepción maintain a faith
beside candles of the Virgin.

Of all the amber prayers cast onto limestone,
not one burns for a flood. We got tired of asking.

Living here goes something like this.

Aren't We All Romantics When We Slumber or Dream?

In the cold and sleek necessity I wait for space,
everything piled back and glowing to 134th Avenue.
There's a radio but it isn't on. There's a clock
but it isn't on time. I carry mistakes with me,
through every inch made of city and night,
where outside the river breathes slow
like an old story about kings and stone.

I have no more money, and brace my restless arm
against the pane of open air,
holding my used book up so I can read in the light
from nearby bars. Their cargo floods out
of their tiny doors and talks loudly of action. A few
crates scream at nothing, like troops coming down
from the lines. I hear someone in another car
scream back, another voice yells *shut up*.

It's inevitable that I'll cross the river, the county line,
the constellations kissing my shoulders and neck
into steel protrusions breaking through the shadows.
In a far country I know there's war and bad water
while here the shiny fish of cars dart through the night,
but the land is losing structures. It's letting me go.

Rob Talbert

Inevitability

Sometime before dawn cracks
the birds begin arriving. They drive
scared bats into early sleep.

Air traffic controllers check and recheck.
The first wave is only scouts, and by the time
you click off the alarm and slide
out of bed, stumbling in the dark
toward the bathroom, branches
and telephone wires already sag
under hollow bones.
You rub your face raw in the shower.
You make coffee and toast.
Legions of wings topple power lines
but in the foggy mirror you pin up your hair,
straighten your tie. Outside,
you find the birds that sit atop
your car weigh more than the car,
and you're only halfway to work
when you can't see the road anymore
through the thickening number of feathers.

You pull onto the shoulder and look
for help, a sign, anything in the chaos.
Up ahead are two brake lights
from another car stopped. A friend.
Someone else trapped.
But in the suffocating flock the red
might have been a cardinal catching
the headlights. Still, you must know for sure.

You place your hand on the door and push
but the birds push back. Holding it closed.
Holding you in.

And there you sit. In your car,
in a city made of birds.
You're supposed to be at work,
at your desk, answering the phone,
but instead you have no choice but to witness
every color and every song already exist.
What more can you do?
What more can you do when you have just one life
and there isn't one new thing left on the earth?

Rob Talbert

Certainty Without the Word *Certainty*

A man approaches the bar. This is a sentence.
His movement and desires for rum. Each step
met with a new word, and how many people
watch him defines the rain of what to call it.

A man approaches the bar (and creates a storm).
I hold avocados in the market and am rephrased
by other shoppers as *a man wishing he'd stayed
in Tijuana.*

A man approaches the bar (and doesn't need
this moment explained). Perhaps the shunning
of better language is just another way we are polite
in public, the inaccuracy intentional. And I was like
see that guy? And he was like *yeah*. And I was like
I bet he's going through some stuff. I don't need
the word *drink* to reach for one, nor *lust*
to be delirious about a woman's hips, but *perfect*
and *careen* and *lever that moves the world* are fine
substitutions for both. When we rolled around
in the night South Dakota grass, that lost-far-away-girl
must solicit other words for rolling around
in the night South Dakota grass. Her hands a different
size than mine, her direction to wind alternate
to my own. The memory is never mindful
of its palace, or place, depending on your affinity
for *a*'s. After all, if only the right memories
and sentences stuck around, our heads
would be a Taj Mahal, which was also built
for a lost-far-away-girl. A man approaches the bar

(and I build a palace in my head.) And I was like *man, this guy must have really been hurt when she died.* And he was like *yeah.*

Rob Talbert

Those Times When a *Thank You* Will Just Have To Do

My mother is dying,
but I still can't forgive her
for the way she treats my father.

I pass through rooms in a cloak
of absolution. I make my peace
with broken love.

Life's preferred pace is a cloud
overhead, hardly noticed
and already leaving.

Five doors in this house
and I only open four.

Alarms blare and work
gobbles me up.
I find my father in its belly,
driving the hammer and never
asking for thanks.

My father passed down to me
a hunger that knows no end.
An oil leak in a body of gears.
An urge to drive forth until
the world unravels.

I look up
and the clouds do not go in reverse.
I wonder if this produces a kind of panic
somewhere within them.

Like when I drive until the gaslight blinks,
then search wildly for a source,
hoarding the fumes.

Job 5: Insurance Certificate Specialist

I try to fly straight through the swarms, through the re-engineered
days of spring in gray cities. I try to hold straight in the gray offices.
In the bomb memory, the explosion of touch and talking with no *boom*
to point to and say "this, here." I hold dear my amorphous concept of self.
It helps illuminate the dark highway before me, held only this for years.

I should have expected the twine holding together the skyscrapers.
And the gum on the cracks of girl's hearts, which is why they chew
so much before sneaking out of bedroom windows. I should have known
the stars were so alluring because even their failure is brilliant. Perfect.
Yet here I am.

Ad Infinitum

There is no end of the world.
The perfection of animals
and the oven of the air endures.
A bird lands on a sill somewhere
when a band takes five, or a radio
dial turns to keep music surviving.
I sleep and the city still changes. I left
school and school kept going. I left
jail and the building still stands,
in the unconquerable heat,
in the contention of guards who've
been there twenty years. My car
knows how to be a car without
my asking. I occupy it and then I
don't, like a job or a side of town.
Nothing ever ends. Not money
or need or the ability of sweat
to bead on the skin.

A few inmates I guarded may still
be locked up in the same cells
with the same plans. I hope
they're out now, landing a job
and hearing what happened
to jazz. If there are no inmates
and no guards then maybe jail
will stop, and the building could
be used to preserve music
by storing bird seed or making
radios. Anything but keeping

people, counting the same days
arriving always from the east.

Night Clubs

I.

It began on Orange Ave where they served free vodka. It began
in a parking lot shotgunning Long Islands.
It began with sex behind the nightclub dumpster. It began with
always
standing in line. I can't be modest and I can't sit still.
Even the moon refills her cup.
Lost days pile up. Build mountains in my past.
I breathe. Alarm clocks scream. The highway rush never stops.
Oh, I know there are real mountains
five seconds through the pulsing doorway.

A woman in a wife-beater and no bra dances arms raised.
Bouncers carry a man outside swinging at every face.
I bum a cigarette from a girl dressed to the slutty 9s.
Someone is puking in the co-ed bathrooms.
Someone on the dance floor becomes a darting sparrow.
Xtacy. Dude in green hat. $10 a hit.
Condoms bloom in the urinal.
The bartenders know me.

Drink me, said the bottle to Alice. *Make me the right size.*
Small enough for keyholes. Large enough to smash the fates.
These are my highways to Elysium: glistening vodka, hilarious rum,
and my pure lover, bourbon, who always *says yes. Pour them, my*
prophetic
and mystic bartender. Saint of internal fire. Savior of countless lives.
My love for you is a snapped power line whipping across the ice.

My heart is a pacing wolf.
In the womb I was built in darkness and now I'm rebuilt in darkness.
I've escaped the uncompromising maw of the world. The start, reverse,
start, reverse of one life already so occupied with sleep. *Grow up. Listen to me.*
You need a man. Be a man. Act your age. Ever thought about kids?
A promotion? What're you doing with that college degree? Think about dieting?
Watch your mouth. Don't be so angry.

They're here by choice, drink by choice, kiss, touch,
dance and fuck and pass out by choice. In this darkness between days
I have not blinked
but I have opened my eyes.

Samantha waits ready to pounce.
My arms are wide.

Escape.
No boss. No parents. No judgment.
No shiny lures, no live bait.
No distraction. No filtration.
You can have it. You can have it tonight.

Take my hand.
Grab hips.
Slide your palm in the small of someone's back.
Fingers through hair
like field mice in the grass.

Escape. Yes.
Break it.
This place.
I am.
Yes.

II.

And what feral engine drives me to inhabit these walls?

The minimum wage shifts that don't just demand your trust
and love
and commitment, but your entire soul. Soaking you in
policies. Blithely
ignoring flat tires, hellish fevers, broken children and sleep.
The cops, teachers, mothers and fathers who lied when they said
you can be
anything you want to be. Denying us the realities of
luck, or that it's all who you know, or that some people
are simply born with angelic gifts.
The choreographed talks in offices of television and sales and
faraway cousins
with needs for a new kidney. Restraining the outside
world to sitcoms and Toronto.
Traffic nearing the density of the sun that sits with you at 5 p.m
upon
the highway, blinding you through the windshield as a
spaceship or heavenly creature would if they'd only
come to get you but never do.
The children screaming in the next aisle of the grocery store for
cartoon cereal

and the mothers who tune out their screams better than
a concentration camp soldier, overflowing out of
electric wheel chairs and huffing through the cold
plastic air for TV dinners.
The pawnshop where Jacob was fired because his car broke
down and made
him late to work three times. Who could fix it if only
the next paycheck would come.
The city jail where the angry drunks and the angry gangbangers
and the angry officers and the angry women with fresh
bruises and black eyes pace around the concrete squares
forever.
The insurance offices where workers stare painfully into glowing
screens, sitting
with their backs to each other, talking out the sides of
their mouths in this brilliant stage of self-evolution.
The unbelievable notion most people carry in their hearts
that they understand and
control the world around them. Who really, truly,
honestly, are not scared to the deepest bone that this is
what their life irrevocably is.

III.

I've found a specter. Behind every door and park bench.
Reminding me
I was promised something else.
Given the keys to a door I cannot find.

I don't know who you are.
Maybe you fucked up.

Spent all your money.
Married or had kids too early,
too late, too trustingly. Gave your best years
to a career that pissed on you.
Had a sex change. Change of heart.
Changed your mind—I don't care.
I stare into the debris of my own actions and cringe.

There are no portals to heaven open during the day,
and I am with you in the same night that existed before the world.
It touched Christ, Buda, Abraham and now ushers us into these
structures.
Watches you stagger to someone else's car.

We can escape together into the deep recess of liquor techno.
You and I can leave behind all unfairness in a fortress of holy
bartenders.
At the Bonham in San Antonio.
At Independent Bar in Orlando.
With the elderly couple on Largo Das Fontes in Madera who
served me Moonbeam shots in the clamor of midnight
Portuguese soap operas.
At Harry's Bar in Paris (bring your wallet).
At the Meet Rack in Tuscan where I hear God is literally waiting.
Our sleep is better off buffered with dreaming than interrupted
with it.

What the world ought to be is as messy
as what it already is.
But we can sip whole countries.
With new contracts. New songs.
Under real stars.

Rob Talbert

Job 6: Corrections Officer

I go through the first door
with a magnetic key. At
the end of a corridor
is another door I open
with a button. I go inside
and say *here, sergeant.*
Then I come to a door
I can't open. A man watching
me through the cameras
in the ceiling opens that door.
I pass through two more doors.
I wait for the man
watching through the cameras
to open the elevator doors.
When those doors open I enter
and say *fourth floor.*
The doors close and then open.
I walk through two more doors.
My job requires the presence
of doors. Walking through doors
is almost the job. I go through
a door into my unit. My station
is an enclosure the size of two
phone booths with two doors.
I take a flashlight and count inmates
behind their doors. There are more
doors than hours in a shift.
More doors than times I reach
for a door. All are made of steel,
even the bathroom door.

Whoever invented jails loved cubes,
felt safety in their completion, closing
off the final section and giving rise
to shape. My unit is a lock-down unit.
I feed inmates through a smaller door
that opens in their door like a mail slot.
A key as big as my hand opens this door.
I am a door. I am a door to I am.
A door to her. To the billowing
sail of her dress in Texas wind.
To the desire for San Antonio nights.
To margaritas and a nightclubs.
I am a door to wishing I never
dropped out of school. To wanting
to know all the constellations.
To being tired of trying
to figure out why these men
strangle their children or burn people
like Kansas plains. Through this door
I'm not fed. I see no guard. I have no window
and I pretend there is no key.
I count nothing of my own.
I never open. I never open.
I can't.

Rob Talbert

A Slow Madness

There are some things you'll never know.

When a tooth will ache.
When a cop will show mercy.
Where a sparrow will dart next,
like some lovers, leaving suddenly.

You'll never know when the heavens
will bless you with rain.
When the past will come knocking.
When money will fill your pockets.

You'll never know the dangers of a forest.
What lies beneath you in the ocean.
What's behind you unless you look.

Still, the masses come running
to scream reason into the still-smoking crater.
And we go back to making sandwiches.
Filling out forms. We fondly imagine
a controllable future. In a world
that never stops eating.

Satellite photos show only
blackness and cold surround this world.
Keeping the stars at a safe distance.
It's obvious we weren't meant
to go anywhere.

The next crowd born
starts the wheel
again.

Rob Talbert

Recap and Apology

—for my sister

I remember darkness inside the car,
and watching you in the night outside.
Both sides of black cradling us like a mother
made of void. I was more restricted,
encased in a toddler's body, and you, the pinball
careening between policemen. Your son
in your hands. I, a son, captive to that theater.

Years later I heard you drove from North Carolina
with the windows down to air out the linen
of your screams about a man giving up,
a man against the river of his own words.
Of all the times you crossed this country
stitched with promises and hope
when have you felt the needles do anything but pierce?

The buildings of any city stand tall and trusting,
and I know you've seen them all, sister. The curves
of St. Louis, labyrinth of Houston, the portal to heaven
in Little Rock. But always the sky is wrecked
at sundown. Always your son grows up and away.
Soon he'll be strong enough to eat you alive.
Some men do it so subtly it will feel like love.

It's Completely Possible Your Grandfather Was a Wolf

Through the dark columns and rustling
houses glow like jack-o-lanterns.
In other woods other houses and insects glow.
Perhaps all woods hold the same amount of light,
as if math and small beacons were distant cousins,
as if the recipe for "night forest" calls for two million lights.

The washing machine is broken again, genesis
and swallower of small oceans. The oranges from the market
know how the wind works but rot consumes them
on the counter.

I have long given up on this town, this way of saying "no,"
of telling the wide world that it's too much to bear,
like turning your back on dreaming, or going home early
from a party. The distant cities run behind these mountains.
The deep waters lap soft ankles.

There's so much proof of bright and distant breathings.
When I abandon the house to wander at night
I leave a lamp on by the window to give the fireflies back their god
while I'm out looking for mine.

It's always quiet enough to hear a plane fly overhead.
I raise my hands to its vast properties, so much closer than I
to a destination, to whatever the Big Dipper holds.
Which has yet to be known.
Which has yet to be spilled.

Rob Talbert

Aria for the Recently Changed

Still awake at 3 a.m.
Still the apartment window
receives all broadcast
from nearby traffic.
So near the rent is cheap.
It never stops. Never retreats.
Blood and information
coursing under halogens
high enough for their own heaven.

Just one car waits beside the road,
emergency lights flashing.
Someone stirred with force enough
to delay destination.
Tell me. If it was you I saw
stopped in the lake-bottom darkness,
could you see my window?
Was your hand cupped loosely
over your mouth or packed into a fist?

Double Dog Dare

Through the heaps of heavy brush
I step with high knees to the porch.
It takes more altitude to get home,
more sky to seep under my shoes
for an uneasy balance.
Even this world has a tilt.
If I put more space into my walk
then I've slightly widened my life,
and eventually I may have room
for a Ferris wheel between the bed
and the bathroom sink, where I stagger
before the ritual of work.
Bring on all things composed of light
and fire. Night is merely something
to crawl into, to expand with yourself
when the day throws in the towel.
Somewhere in a stadium a coach
tells her players to keep going.
In the dim apartment glow, a man
is tying his shoes. Even now
someone has smashed berries
and smeared them into the sky.
All I do is own things, but I'm also
the thousand uses people and things
make of me, and I shine each purpose
until my skin competes with the moon.
The clock, after all, is ticking,
and these are the 3 abandoned acres
of a friend now dead. I watch the brush
crumple, blaze and become wild.

If you learn to start fires you'll learn
how much fight you've got in you.
To all fates, all gods, all demons:
come and get me.

En Route

This is the lifetime of my long shadow,
outstretched and going on walks
of its own. Somewhere a car struggles
to start. It interrupts the seconds,
the beckoning crickets.

A bus goes by,
that sluggish box of light
anyone can open,
growing smaller on its way
until it looks like a star,
and I forget who I am
or where I am going.

Homes stand aligned in the darkness.
Wind pushes me sideways
and down another street
as if I am breaking some law,
as if to say, *trust me,*
there's nothing for you over there.

Rob Talbert

Cloudcroft

The pipes refroze every night. We tried tying bows
on them with bathroom towels, held flames to their bellies
like cigarettes, I believed in the soul—
nothing worked. Nothing worked except winter.

Her family kept to themselves. I cut firewood by the barn
and slept in the basement, and at night I could hear them
        walking
out a map in every room. The soft voices trickling down through
the wood, an aquifer of sound. *He's just a phase* pooled down to me

from the kitchen. The cranky metal of the furnace kept time,
        clicking
from the blaze inside that had nothing to do with wood
or the metronome swing of an axe. Its belly expanding,
millimeters closer to my army cot. We kept right on living.

The last week my girlfriend's uncle melted
snow on the stove to keep the toilets running for the women.
I climbed the stairs in the familiar cold, pressed open
the screen door that whined about my exit though no one

woke up or got out of bed, and from the porch I peed onto the
        snow.
A freezing breeze blew over the house and headed for the dark,
misshapen mass of the woodpile.
Even from the cabin I could see the handle

of the axe sticking up from the ground. The wind disappeared
into the trees beyond the barn. It was quieter than sleep.

You Their Cipher

I didn't build my own house.
My wife isn't friends with the wife
of the man who drove nails into the doorway
so I can define inside and outside easily.
That warrants a *thank you*, I think.

It's easier to forget what day it is
than how I live. Machines made
my furniture, so I have no guilt
moving a desk across the room and whether
the person who built it intended it
for underneath a window. Perhaps
I'm just looking for accountability.

If I build a birdhouse I like thinking
about the kind of bird that will live in it.
A small blue thing, rather than the nest
of wasps that will take it over.
And I like thinking I've accidentally imagined
someone perfectly in some damp country
walking along the soft roads; that what I meant
to be fabricated was actually a whole body and heart.
What is made goes away from its maker.
On some level this is natural: kids leave home,
things are sold or fly away. But in every city
there are some lights that never turn off.
I wish more of my friends were like that.
They never turn out how I plan.
I mean, really, only the people who burry
time capsules dig them back up.

Rob Talbert

Not Honesty but Something Like It

The weather is often on my mind. I desire
change in most things but then everything would need
renaming. I bow my head when I can't think of
a better

word for *sky*, and I can't remember ever
looking in the mirror and saying my own name;
wishing the glass did more than simply give the
whole world
back. It has no responsibility.

I have to do
more than these walls. The safely mundane topics
of short drives and lost receipts. I need to return
more

than a sweater but first I need to find some other
way to wear it: to stay warm and still allow the winter
sunshine to lick my skin, reminding my whole
body

that even though it was built in darkness it
was meant to be seen.

Who invented rivers and called
them the difference between your side and mine? Gravity
whispers to them any direction it chooses.
I stand on my side of the bank and ask everything what
it is.

30 Minutes In a Small Town and 30 Minutes Only

I can't understand the woman at McDonalds.
She weaves a tangled lace of South Carolina
vowels; an accent like strong coffee.
There's a firework store next door. Food
and bombs in a town stitched together
with abandoned grocery carts. I order food.
Three college students behind me are whispering,
making fun of the woman. She says *can't*
like *cain't* and *order* like *awder*. I take
my burger outside and sit on the curb under
the red neon bottle rocket. A huge sign under
a huge sky over a small town. Had I been born
here, I'd work here. Supply the town with things
to send up into the clouds. I wouldn't be what I am:
a stranger, a tourist road weary and never
coming back. My car wouldn't be boiling oil
with Texas plates. I'd be the guy at the fireworks
store. I'd know every spark and crackle of light
a fuse would lead to. I'd have a South Carolina
shadow, and maybe a daughter. My speech
would have more bird inside it, if I was here.
Who would I love in this town? How often
would I get arrested or eat at the Waffle House?
The three students come out of the McDonalds
screaming and laughing and pile into the car.
I watch them go, watch them turn onto I-95
and speed off. Their red taillights weaken
and recede up the hill like a climbing flame.

Soon I will follow them and abandon everyone here.
I will never return and my betrayal will
be perfect. When fireworks come back to earth
they come back changed.

Confessions in a College Town

Slurred speech is a jazz that never kissed vinyl.
Oh, how I talk abundantly near the kitchen table
where the red Solo cups crouch in little columns,
and the kegs or bottles get grabbed eagerly
like shoeboxes filled with God.

Parents go insane with hope in a college town,
dreaming their little dumbbells:
their kids calculating velocities in the WalMart lamplight,
bean bags never sticking with the sweat of sex,
or washing machines replacing parties.

I watch young girls in high heels stagger
down ancient sidewalks. Their asses framed by dresses
and the ideas they had when the little zippers slid up.

I watch young men moving in packs between the bars
and the frat houses, stealing kisses from other men
in the safety of their drunkenness.

I watch chaos in dorm hallways. Puke splatter
like Pollack paintings. The smell of weed and hookah
billowing to the bass of heartbeats and rap.

The mind would weigh more than the earth
if each *want* was a small piece of iron.
I hear often from the locals that this town is sinking.

Rob Talbert

Job 7: Unemployed

I walk out of the Home Depot in a shirt and tie.
The pavement I'm crossing shrugs off what heat
that it can, warping the world that passes
through its emissions.

The Home Depot chases after me. I can hear the beeping
of forklifts in reverse, a manager yelling
and registers slamming closed. I can still smell the pine beams
that collapsed onto the floor in thunderous crashes.

Should my speech be damaged somewhere by gravity or disease,
I imagine drawing a picture or moving my hands
in the fashion of what I craved. I try to make my hands
into a lake or rain, yet all I manage is a gesture like playing
a falling piano.

If the manager calls me back
it will be for a fourth interview. *I have a stomach*
and require food that necessitates money
which is why I have a tie and hope I get this job is something
I shouldn't say in an interview but it's accurate for why I am there.

I never know anyone with something going on and I'm uncertain
if this is a failure of how I speak to people. I don't know anyone
who's been laid off from work while the economy has been
drinking
for years, sitting on the edge of the valley. I don't know anyone
with cancer, or anyone who's been to war and talks about it.
I suddenly start walking in a manner that suggests I have
somewhere to go.

The car is heavy with heat, is almost pure light and fire.
At the other end of the parking lot a policeman
is standing in the middle of an intersection directing traffic.
He moves his hands in ways the drivers recognize. All of it
is a big dance: This means *come here*. This means *you wait*.
This means *I've watched you for years*.

Rob Talbert

Honing

Eventually the body
gets robbed of its push.
This can take years.
A slow and patient madness

swelling from the inside
like an understanding,
like a memory with teeth.
All days will come.

All debts will be paid.
All anger will surface.
My vessel can sail
only so far in these waters

and then will kiss
the dark and cold bottom,
as this world kisses
the dark and cold surrounding it.

I must light my candles.
I sing a brash and jagged tune
because I must sing something
in this play with no second act.

Even birds go silent in heavy rain.
I get my call into the air
before it leaks out,
and the body is genius at leaking.

The blood turns over and over.
The sun rises. These are among
few things guaranteed, like wishes
dragged into the grave

and the next wave.

Rob Talbert

Driving to Virginia for a Job that Paid Minimum Wage

I leave my wife and drive all day,
then I sleep outside some diner in Birmingham.
Through all six states a trail of apple cores
go out like flares from the window
until my old apartment takes shape around
me. I put things back where I get them.

I look for the promises of my parents
and teachers. I look on the back
of my degrees like there're instructions
I missed. Stories of home wash over my back
in the morning showers. My friends smoke Marlboros
to send what signals they can between apartments
and bookstore jobs and nursing home jobs.

If my wife's face is an ocean my eyes
have often gone sailing. But I've docked
too far for anything but a phone to be sufficient,
rolling around in my pocket while I smile
at customers strolling about the store.

I feel like a president, not America's, but another one
in some other country I've never heard of, saving
a small treasury of nickels and spectacular views of the ocean
while powerful foreign ships loom off the coast.
How shall I keep my already divided empire?
Sutures require such exact materials and technique.
Today is the fourth of July.

You Jumped

—for Erica Smith

I read comic books as a kid because I wanted to fly
more than anything, stay high above the molten
rivers of night traffic and learn whether living
without ground meant I'd never again take
touch for granted. Of course, there's always
the chance of falling—a fear that's kept me
off diving boards my whole life and bungee cords
with bridges attached to them. Erica went skydiving
before she went drinking. This was long after
the rush hour of high-school classes carried her
face out the door and into the city of our twenties. A face
I still recognized on the front page of the newspaper.
Maybe I was in love with her, the only woman
I was sure had fallen to earth smiling and screaming,
who stepped out of the safety metal can give us
and opened her arms across the vast green-tiled floor
planes look down upon, the loud roar of progress
in her ears, touch now a language only wind can
speak. Maybe the man driving the other car
that night was a pilot, wishing for more directions,
wishing for wings the way I did in the obscurity
of youth, wrapped in the walls of my bedroom and
crouched over superheroes. Cities can give you
everything. A bed made of street so reassuringly solid,
and all the sky you can take in, before someone picks
you up and it falls out of you.

Rob Talbert

Watching

Streetlights flicker on and tighten their grip.
Some people feel followed. Chased out of malls

by security guards into dense and reflective traffic.
The city's skin stares right back. It doesn't matter

that it's snowed for days, that snow has followed us
into all structure: Charlie shelves aluminum cans

under white hair. It's snowing in his past.
There are still miracles to get our hands on,

but a hornet's nest of bills stirs on the table
and the tumbling candlelight sends

shadows grasping from the dark. Who sees
the drop of water escape down the bowl, the stem,

the base? It could be the flake on your shoulder.
We are still here.

Being a Boomerang I Threw at Myself

My friends build me a castle made of sadness.
They're all moving apartments, trying for kids
and applying for better jobs—no word yet.

I left San Antonio and suffer my own absence.
I need to come back with the months of last year
spilling from my canvas bag. I need to be predictable
in movements other than leaving. I get up
to use the bathroom. Pablo's house is rich
with posters of Picasso paintings, framed and clean
as cold water. I piss into the toilet and stare
at a picture I know is the bombing
of some country but I don't know which one
or when or what to call it. I'm not a reliable narrator;
I've had too much to drink. And I'm not ashamed
of wanting to kiss my best friend's wife
the way I kiss my own wife, nor if my wife kissed him.

Please forgive me my city,
my concrete and electric womb,
for now I'm just a visitor, a print of something
more original. But my friends are still there,
drinking and smoking into the lace of summer.
Outside the garage and beyond them I watch
the edge of night creep closer to our chairs
like a cat so black its shadow lights the way.

Rob Talbert

Job 8: Corrections Officer

I have never seen a wild thing.
Not the smoke billowing from the house
down the street, lit up last night
like a jack-o'-lantern, waist-high flames
tearing into the night. And certainly not
the man in cell 17, who can say from experience
how many times a knife should plunge into flesh
before death is imminent. There are rules to these
kinds of things. Murder is never wild: You choose
who, hold the weapon like *this*, then execute.
Fire is the same way. House plus electrical problem
equals neighbors standing outside in bathrobes.
You could build religion on this kind of certainty.

Guards live by the faith of numbers. At the jail
I count all the mops and brooms, then the inmates
pacing concrete. Four killers, nine wife beaters, six
thieves. Jail itself is not wild either. They watch TV
and I watch them, I eat first and then they eat, more
TV, then showers, medication, the cold river stone
of the moon rises in the window, and they rack up.
What is wild is the gaze of the inmate, which is
confined to nothing and tracks you for miles
like a wolf. What's wild is their whispering, which
goes unchecked and carries the judgment of killers.
What is wild is their closed fist, which I have met
deep in the church of speed and precision, and will
meet again and again, amen. New inmate today,
a tall Mexican man held together by tattoos. He
hands me a card with a picture of him twelve minutes

younger. Underneath it says ARSON, and I ask
where were you last night?

Rob Talbert

Having the Nerve

While you were asleep
the world changed.

Deep fissures pushed
the monuments around.
All skies recalibrated.
Love was made and unmade.
The wine blew the doors
right off their hinges.
A bullet train of old hope
shot through the city.
Every living thing lost more time.

Most people look down
or right over the tall parks.
They're not dead
but their hearts are in port.
Waiting. The wind
and currents useless around
them, which is a kind of dying.

You sleep, and somewhere
a light goes on.
You sleep while someone else
tallies it up:

A door handle is the most
common thing let go. Next
come the hours, let go
without conscience.

Then ideas are let go.
Then coins. Then hope,
then love, then lovers.
After that we let go of wine.
Then pride. Then the past.
Until the last thing remaining is desire.

A bird keeps coming back
to the balcony. I keep coming back
to mortality. The wind
forever comes back.

You speak above molten rivers.
You traverse a tilted blue marble.
What could be missed more
than this space to act? What remains
when you tally it up for yourself?

Let the body be pulled forth
and emerge. Follow the white rabbit
into the soft and suffocating
grace of city nights.
Dance for long hours.
Keep the fires burning.
Know well that someday
all rooms will fill with water.

Rob Talbert

The Night the Last Drive-In Closed

The owner died a few hours before
the storm came in from the gulf.
All shove and saltwater crazy.
We were drunk and on YouTube
when thunder shook power
from off the walls and left us
scrambling for candles. Either way
it wasn't going to happen. We'd cancelled
on our friends much earlier;
It was a night I didn't feel like hiding
in a trunk, rolling back and forth
on the flat spare tire while the car
inched up in line. There surely
would've been a fistfight,
then a small Mexican boy going car to car
selling candy, then we'd all place
our grief on the dashboard,
then all the plastic Rosaries
hanging from rearview mirrors
would get caught up
in bare feet and M&Ms.

The rain kept everyone out,
kept us from spilling out of walls and cars.
The news said when a stroke
bullied its way into his head,
the sun still bled in through the blinds.

I imagine in the distance from *head rush*
to *collision with living room carpet*

his life went off like a movie,
all 87 years of frame and girls.
Going off steady as the flash of streetlights
on the way home, beaming through
backseat windows, replacing stars
in busy cities. It didn't matter
that we stayed home. Nothing matters
when a fight comes looking for you:
a storm knocking out the power,
some jealous lover, a stroke
dragging thoughts from your body.
Anything to muddy the earth
you've parted so long with your own hands.

Rob Talbert

Caution

Arctic Terns cross the earth
for 30 years. Monarchs tumble into Texas
and the oceans swell with great distance.

It appears it's okay to feel tired
once and a while. Hang it up and return
to a dimly lit room that still needs cleaning.

I sleep and the city grinds steady outside
with factory shifts and cops,
pregnancy and false laughter.

It's better to keep charged up
but hope is a AA battery.
It's easier to starve than pay the rent,
but I don't want to die young.

People live blindly in streets made of light.
They ignore long shadows telling them they're giants.

My stripped cogs fall back into place.
I pledge the rest of my life at job interviews.
What I thought were whole chapters of my past
were only false starts. Sentences I've crossed out.

But there is a rare pack of animals prowling
through the alleys. Invisible. Hunting only the fire
that burns in the chest. They migrate
up and down the grid, looking for new prey.

If you were born into this world
you've been mauled by one.

Rob Talbert

River Mind

A river is more than a place to drown
twisting underneath and around highways,
keeping watch on idling cars
heavy with *they did them wrong*.
You can enter this space but you can't
survive long. A river throws back what it can.
Pushing lights into their own source.
Sending faces back onto the carnivals
who cast them.

A river becomes 10,000 voices
all chanting no.
The barges press down and the river says no.
Under the full moon's abusive blade
the river says no. Beside the city, between the city,
in cheap postcards of the city,
I watch every stitch of color and body
caught and repelled back into air.
I stare down
from hotel windows or the sides
of dim bridges drunk on low fog.
Perhaps all the reflections, the throwing back,
the infinite rejection isn't *no*, but *know*.
A river language in a river mind.
Know this bar light is green.
No, you need it more than I.
Know your face distorted by boats
and fantastic wind. No, it doesn't belong
with sticks. Cradle my forgetfulness,
river, return the words I didn't to hear.

The perfumes I failed to reward.
The lips I missed on the way
to another conversation.
Warp the inaccurate world into a scene
showing me all twists and traps.

I turn back to my steel ecstasy of noise.
Keeping a level head. Where I always
try to run steady, clear and cool.

Rob Talbert

The Land Runs Out

Wind brings the coast back to me.

It's been five years
since the corner apartment,
chasing out mice in the single lamplight.
Outside the restaurant
I'm slapped with a briny, humid tumbling.

An edge has found me in the high city.
In the spinning fog of buying, sleeping, trying,
eating, working, working.
An edge to look over and see
no god and no palm tree
where the mind ends.

Sometimes the edge is a rooftop.
Other times it's a knife.
An edge is a lover or the money running out.

I jog down Ennis-Joslin at 1 a.m.

until the dark and roaring waves
sing *go back, you've been beaten.*

My past has an edge and that edge is me.
Where it ceases to be a dream
or lost, which is what dreams are.

Not much more can be done. How easily
a web is destroyed by wind.
A home by normal living.

Rob Talbert

Birthday Party

The cigarettes make a cumulus of this kitchen.
I want one but know where it leads:
same as where anything craved leads: to getting cornered.

No one's allowed upstairs. The basset wanders around
with his long nails tapping on the tile like a clock.
Gone are most guests, the chips, our voices, the night

now melting into 6 a.m. blue, but fragments linger,
in the bowl or the lipstick smudged on the edge of a glass.

Sometimes it feels like everything just hangs on.
Twisting and shifting to keep the fountain flowing.

How thin is the line between survivor and relic?
Between yes and too late? Days and dreams and dogs

all pass into irretrievable reservoirs. I hear the furnace boom,
then shudder, a train going nowhere.

Galloping

A scene of constant tearing
stares back onto the porch.
Talons enter flesh. Flesh enters mouths.
This happens without mercy.
Without guilt.

I can never leave the apartment
in this exact body,
this precise thought, but not because
of what waits in the trees.
I take shelter in a forest of memory.
I'm here and twelve years old
kissing a girl in church. In the dark streets
of Stratford closing the phone booth door.
In Texas, in a car, my sister
is swarmed by cops. Life is something
merely traded. Explored and given back
like a lover's body.
The moon possesses a kind of stealth
others reserve for crime. Nailed to all our lives.
It holds on as we hold on, as the blunt weapon
of the world smashes into the future.
A backyard party rolls nearby on loose axles.
From there comes a cry, and a kiss,
a hive of slipped attempts.
Police lights open their eyes.
The moon listens from so high up
all our whispers make one song.

Rob Talbert

Nocturne

I watch everyone around the table
have a smile the shape of a different country.
We belong to the ruins: Industrialization is over.
If there's a future to be had we cannot build it.
If tomorrow looms it isn't because of steel.
The Golden Gate Bridge is now just a hyphen
between California and the world swallowing California.
And in this old house the creaking pine floor
beneath my feet is my friend's midnight aria
on his thirsty walk to the fridge. This is how we live
with stability. Tonight we have coals to smoke through,
and whiskey to keep us warm, and fireworks
for the sky to wear like jewelry.

I've been drinking three hours now and have
become a wind-up bird. On the other side
of the house another friend buys pizza
from a station wagon that shakes in order
to stay together. Any car is more beautiful
than an earthquake, even one that sounds
like an earthquake. It's a rolling museum of hands
and smelting, of families and their efforts to have
what they make in factories. The night is all of us leaving
at the same time, is how our era is over,
is how we are pulled apart to different places
and time zones. The semester is over.
The Industrial Era is over. The night is.
The night is a dark dress I don't want
to see slip off. It's much too close
to the only thing I have in place of goodbye.

ACKNOWLEDGEMENTS

Many thanks are due to the editors and readers of the following publications where these poems first appeared, some in different forms.

2River Review: "You Jumped"

Adroit: "Recap and Apology"

American Poetry Review: "Job 1: Corrections Officer," "Job 8: Corrections Officer" (originally published as "Cell Door"), "Deviation Insures Failure"

Bare Root Review: "Confessions in a College Town"

Boxcar Poetry Review: "What Practice Makes"

BoySlut: "Cruise Ship Room Attendant," "Storming the Gates"

Front Porch: "Me Being a Boomerang I Threw at Myself"

Inkwell: "The Night the Last Drive-In Closed"

Keyhole: "Cherries Becoming More Like Cherries," "You Their Cipher," "30 Minutes In a Small Town and 30 Minutes Only"

LA Review of LA: "Announcements," "Night Clubs"

Mad Hatters' Review: "Baggage," "Birthday Party"

Ninth Letter: "Crusoe, Wistful"

Painted Bride Quarterly: "The Last Scene in Casablanca"

Poet Lore: "Aren't We All Romantics When We Slumber or Dream?"

The Portland Review: "Not Honesty but Something Like It"

Southern Poetry Review: "En Route"

The Sow's Ear Review: "Cloudcroft"

ABOUT THE AUTHOR

Rob Talbert grew up in the sweltering heat of San Antonio and spent most nights playing in bands or dancing in nightclubs. He has worked in jails, bars, corporate offices, hotels, universities, hospitals, retail stores, restaurants and on cruise ships. In 2010 he received his MFA from Virginia Tech University, and he is currently working on a Ph.D. in Creative Writing at Florida State University. His poems have appeared in *Alaska Quarterly, The American Poetry Review, Ninth Letter, Painted Bride Quarterly, Passages North, Southern Poetry Review, Sou'wester,* and on *Verse Daily*. He currently lives in Tallahassee with his wife, Samantha.

www.ingramcontent.com/pod-product-compliance
Lightning Source LLC
Chambersburg PA
CBHW022159080426
42734CB00006B/499
9781941196113